MYSTERIOUS DISAPPEARANCES

D0528271

John Townsend

Raintree

www.raintreepublishers.co.uk
Visit our website to find out more information about Raintree books.

To order:
☎ Phone 44 (0) 1865 888113
🖹 Send a fax to 44 (0) 1865 314091
💻 Visit the Raintree Bookshop at www.raintreepublishers.co.uk to browse our catalogue and order online.

First published in Great Britain by Raintree Publishers, Halley Court, Jordan Hill, Oxford OX2 8EJ, part of Harcourt Education Ltd. Raintree is a registered trademark of Harcourt Education Ltd.

© Harcourt Education Ltd 2004
First published in paperback in 2005.
The moral right of the proprietor has been asserted.

Editorial: Charlotte Guillain and Isabel Thomas
Design: Michelle Lisseter and Bridge Creative Services Ltd
Picture Research: Maria Joannou and Kay Altwegg
Production: Jonathan Smith

Originated by Ambassador
Printed and bound in China

ISBN 1 844 43218 1 (hardback)
08 07 06 05 04
10 9 8 7 6 5 4 3 2 1

ISBN 1 844 43228 9 (paperback)
09 08 07 06 05
10 9 8 7 6 5 4 3 2 1

British Library Cataloguing in Publication Data
Townsend, John, 1924
Mysterious disappearances. – (Out there)
1. Disappearances (Parapsychology) – juvenile literature
2. Alien abduction – Juvenile literature
001.9'4

A full catalogue record for this book is available from the British Library.

Acknowledgements
Page 5, Photodisc/; 4, PA Photos/Sean Dempsey; 6–7, Corbis/James A. Sugar; 6 left, Corbis/Maiman Rick; 7 right, Mark Wagner/aviation-images.com; 8–9, Getty Images Stone/; 8 left, Science Photo Library/Sinclair Stammers; 9 right, Corbis/; 10 right, Bill Bachman/; 10 left, Corbis/Bettmann; 11, Corbis/Bettmann; 13, Hulton Getty/; 14–15, Island Focus/Sue Anderson; 14, Island Focus/Sue Anderson; 15, Photodisc/; 17, Popperfoto/; 16 left, Robert Harding/J Jackson; 18, Corbis/Bisson Bermard; 18–19, Science Photo Library/Worldsat International Inc; 19, Science Photo Library/; 21, Corbis/Bettmann; 20, Corbis/Ralph A. Clevenger; 21, Kos Picture Source/; 22–23, Naval Historical Foundation/; 23, Aviation Images/; 22, Corbis/Dennis Degnan; 24–25, Corbis/Jack Fields; 24 left, Science Photo Library/Worldsat International Inc & J Knighton; 25, Robert Harding; 26, Robert Harding/M Alexander; 27, Corbis/Bettmann; 28 bottom, Corbis/Bettmann; 29, Corbis/Bettmann; 28 top, Corbis/Bettmann; 30 top, Cobis/; 30 bottom, Popperfoto/; 31, Corbis/Rykoff Collection; 33, Newspix/Nationwide News, Australia; 32 right, Popperfoto/; 32 left, Corbis/Eric and David Hosking; 34–35, Mountain Camera/John Cleare; 34 left, Mountain Camera/John Cleare; 35, Corbis/Bolante Anthony; 37 right, Getty Images Taxi/; 36 left, Fretwater Press/; 36–37, Corbis/Pat O'Hara; 39, Corbis/Bettmann; 39, Corbis/Bettmann; 40–1, Corbis/Terry W. Eggers; 41, Corbis/Owaki –Kulla; 40 left, Corbis/Adam Woolfitt; 42–43, Corbis/Brian A. Vikander; 43, Associated Press/; 42, Corbis/; 46, Corbis/Massimo Mastrorillo; 46–47, Corbis; 47, Mountain Camera/John Cleare; 49 left, Ronald Grant Archive/; 48, Corbis/Pat O'Hara; 49 right, Corbis/; 50–51, Anthony Blake Picture Library/; 51, NHPA/; 50, Corbis/Chris Collins; 45, Australian Associated Press/; 44, Associated Press/; 44–45, Associated Press/. Cover photograph reproduced with permission of Robert Harding Picture Library.

Every effort has been made to contact copyright holders of any material reproduced in this book. Any omissions will be rectified in subsequent printings if notice is given to the publishers.

Disclaimer
All the Internet addresses (URLs) given in this book were valid at the time of going to press. However, due to the dynamic nature of the Internet, some addresses may have changed, or sites may have changed or ceased to exist since publication. While the author and Publishers regret any inconvenience this may cause readers, no responsibility for any such changes can be accepted by either the author or the Publishers.

CONTENTS

WITHOUT TRACE   4

WHATEVER HAPPENED?   6

INTO THIN AIR   12

THE BERMUDA TRIANGLE   18

MORE DEVIL'S TRIANGLES   24

KIDNAP OR MURDER?   28

ACCIDENT OR MORE?   34

LOST AND FOUND   40

FACT OR FICTION?   48

FIND OUT MORE   52

GLOSSARY   54

INDEX   56

Any words appearing in the text in bold, **like this**, are explained in the Glossary. You can also look out for them in the Weird words box at the bottom of each page.

WITHOUT TRACE

PLAYING DEAD

Some people **fake** their own death or go missing to escape from their past. They may want to fool:

- the police
- a gang
- an **assassin**
- the secret service
- the tax office
- a nagging partner!

So they disappear forever...

In the time it takes you to read this page, someone will be reported missing. Each day hundreds of people around the world disappear.

Many will turn up somewhere soon. Others may be found after a long time. But some will never be seen again. They vanish from the face of the Earth forever. Or so it seems.

Dear Sue,
I'm leaving you. Don't try looking for me. You'll never find me. I'm starting a new life in South America...

MISSING

HAVE YOU SEEN RICHARD?

Richard, aged 24, was last seen in his office in Oxford at around 4 pm Friday 13 October.
He is 6ft 1ins tall of average build with short brown hair and a freckle on his left cheek.

When last seen, he was wearing a blue and white striped shirt and black trousers.

Anyone with information as to his whereabouts should contact Police.

WHERE?

Strange cases still baffle the experts. Where do 'the disappeared' go? These mysteries have puzzled the world for years. What happens to 'the lost'? Who are the **victims**?

A missing person poster can sometimes help to find people. **‹‹**

WEIRD WORDS   assassin   killer who hunts down a victim
fake   not real

WHY?

Most people who go missing have a reason.
It could be one of the following.

- Perhaps they run away to start a new life.
- Perhaps they are unwell, need help or forget who they are.
- Perhaps they are taken by other people. Kidnappings do happen. Sometimes they even end in murder.
- Perhaps they get lost, go the wrong way, fall or get stuck. It may take ages for a search party to find them.

Now and again a whole group of people vanishes. No reasons or clues are left behind. Will we ever solve these real mysteries of the disappeared?

> Sometimes people run away. But this cannot explain every mysterious disappearance. **》**

FIND OUT LATER...

Why will some mysteries never be solved?

Why do some places have a bad reputation?

Why did this person disappear?

victim   person who gets hurt or killed

WHATEVER HAPPENED?

NO APPARENT REASON

In 1975, Jackson Wright drove with his wife to New York City through the Lincoln Tunnel. He stopped the car to wipe the windscreen. When he got back inside, his wife had gone. He had heard nothing. Martha Wright had simply vanished, never to be found again.

Jackson Wright swore his wife disappeared outside the tunnel. Police found no signs of a struggle.

It seems unreal that a person can be here one minute and gone the next. Can they just disappear, never to be seen again? It happened to a man called Jerrold Potter in 1968.

OVER MISSOURI

A passenger aeroplane was flying from Kankakee in Illinois to Dallas in Texas. It was a clear summer day. During the flight Mrs Potter saw her husband Jerrold make his way to the back of the plane to use the toilet. She never saw him again.

After waiting some time, she asked one of the staff to check if he was all right. When they looked, the toilet was empty. He was nowhere on the plane.

WEIRD WORDS   cabin   room for passengers or crew on an aircraft

OPEN DOOR

The rear door of the aeroplane was just open. This did not suck out the air from inside the plane, like it would in modern aircraft. That is because the **cabin** was not **pressurized** as it would be today. A chain for keeping the door shut was found on the floor.

Had Jerrold Potter bumped into the door and fallen out of the plane? To do this, he would have needed to turn a big door handle that was hard to move. No one saw or heard him fall.

So what did happen to Jerrold Potter? A long search was made along the aeroplane's flight path. His body was never found. The mystery remains to this day.

How could someone disappear from a flying aeroplane?

EXIT

Could Jerrold have mistaken the exit door for the toilet?

Everyone has a unique DNA pattern.

FINDING THE MISSING

When the police find human remains, how can they **identify** them? Now the police can quickly match the details of a missing person with a dead body. **Databases** of dental records or **DNA** information can help solve many mysteries. This was not possible a few years ago.

MISSING IN THE NIGHT SKY

The man wore a suit and tie. He carried a briefcase and wore sunglasses. He said his name was Dan Cooper. He bought a ticket for a one-way flight from Portland to Seattle in the USA. It was November, 1971.

What happened to the passenger called Dan Cooper is a great mystery. After the plane had taken off, he handed a note to the stewardess. The note said that he had a bomb. He said the crew had to land at Seattle and pick up $200,000 and four parachutes. The crew followed his orders and the passengers got off, unaware of the **drama**. The plane took off once more with just the crew and Cooper on board.

database   computer records for sorting information quickly
DNA   code locked in our genes that makes us who we are

STORMY NIGHT

With the cash tied to his body and a parachute on his back, Cooper jumped from the plane over 3 kilometres (2 miles) up. The night outside was freezing. The wind chill made it 70 °C below zero. Could he **survive** in only a raincoat? Cooper and his parachute were never found. Did he die or did he get away with it?

In 1980 a boy found $5880 in decaying bank notes by the Columbia River, north-west of Vancouver. They matched those given to Cooper. Maybe he was killed in the jump, but no evidence has ever been found. And what happened to the rest of the cash? No one knows.

The Columbia River may hide the missing $194,120.

UNSOLVED MYSTERY

Did Cooper fall in the Columbia River? After his disappearance he even became something of a hero. A film of his story came out ten years later. In 2000, a woman in Florida said her dying husband confessed to being Cooper. We will never know the truth now.

identify   find out someone's name
survive   stay alive

Harold Holt was the 22nd prime minister of Australia. The **official** record said:

Harold Holt – born in Sydney in 1908. Prime Minister for less than two years. Died in Melbourne in 1967 (presumed drowned).

The mystery now seems to be forgotten.

MISSING IN THE SEA

The news stunned the world. Australia's prime minister was missing. Harold Holt vanished on 17 December 1967. He has never been found.

Harold Holt was a fit and lively 59-year-old. He was a good swimmer, too. As always, he had run down the beach for his morning swim. No one saw if he plunged into the heavy surf that day. It all happened at Cheviot Beach, Victoria, where the huge waves crash on to the sand. Only a strong swimmer could handle the sea there. Not many people were about and no one saw what happened. Harold Holt was never seen again. Soon the quiet beach was full of police.

Harold Holt vanished on this beach in Australia.

official   according to the rules and records
rumour   story based on gossip

MASSIVE HUNT

The air, land and sea search began that afternoon. It went on for days, but no **trace** of the prime minister was found.

There were many **rumours** about the vanished man. People said his job had been too much for him. Perhaps he had plotted his own disappearance. Maybe he wanted to get away from it all and start a new life. Others said he was a spy and a submarine had taken him away!

Perhaps he was not as fit as he thought he was. Was he swept out to sea? Did the waves crash him into rocks? Did a shark get him? It is unlikely now that the world will ever know.

The Glenn Miller band became even more famous when their leader disappeared.

trace   sign, track or footprint

INTO THIN AIR

FROM THE LOG OF THE DEI GRATIA, DECEMBER 5, 1872

'Seeing no one on deck, I sent the mate and two men on board. They returned in about an hour and reported the ship to be the *Mary Celeste* from New York. It was abandoned with three feet of water in the **hold**.'

One famous vanishing mystery is of the **deserted** ship, the *Mary Celeste*. The mystery has never been solved and probably never will.

The ship set sail from New York in 1872. It had a crew of seven men. The American captain was called Benjamin Briggs. He had his wife and two-year-old daughter with him. The ship was heading for Genoa in Italy. It was carrying a **cargo** of alcohol across the Atlantic Ocean. A few days later the ship was seen drifting near Portugal.

Sailors from another American sailing ship called the *Dei Gratia* climbed aboard the empty *Mary Celeste*. The ship's decks and sails were wet after recent storms. The lifeboat had gone.

NORTH AMERICA

New York

EUROPE

Genoa

AFRICA

The *Mary Celeste's* route. The X marks the spot where it was found. »

cargo   goods carried on a ship or aircraft
deserted   left empty

We will never know what happened to this ship.

WHY DID THEY LEAVE THE SHIP?

- Pirates? Nothing was stolen.
- Illness? Why would they ALL leave?
- Fighting? There was no blood or signs of **violence**.
- Bad weather? They would have been safer staying on the ship.
- Dangerous cargo? Everything was safe and in order.

NO CLUES

There was no sign of a struggle on board the *Mary Celeste*. Yet the ten people who had been on the ship had vanished. They were never seen again. Captain Briggs was a good sailor with a lot of experience. Why would he order everyone to abandon ship? Nothing in the **ship's log** gave any clues. So what made them leave in a hurry?

For years people have asked what happened to the ship's passengers, as well as the lifeboat. Did it sink? Did they land on an island and die of thirst? Did a sea creature or a storm finish them off? The truth is, we will never know.

New York, Nov 3rd 1872

My dear Mother
It seems real homelike since Sarah and Sophia got here, and we enjoy our little quarters... Our vessel is in beautiful trim and I hope we shall have a fine passage but I have never been in her before and can't say how she'll sail.
Hoping to be with you in the spring with much love
I am yours affectionately
Benj

An extract from Captain Briggs' last letter, written on board the *Mary Celeste*.

---

hold   space in the lower part of a ship for storing the **cargo**
ship's log   diary written up each day by the captain

AT THE EDGE OF THE HEBRIDES

Of all the Scottish islands, Eilean Mor is the most mysterious. It was said to be haunted by the dead sailors lost in its dangerous waters. The lighthouse is 24 km (15 miles) west of the Isle of Lewis. It still flashes every 30 seconds.

Eilean Mor is quiet but mysterious.

THE ISLAND OF THE DEAD

The small Scottish island of Eilean Mor had a new lighthouse. Three men lived and worked in the lighthouse to warn ships away from rocks. Lighthouses were not **automatic** then.

On Boxing Day, 1900, the supply boat called at the island as it did every two weeks. It brought food and picked up one of the lighthouse keepers for his leave. But this time there was something wrong. The new 25-metre-high lighthouse was deathly quiet. There was no sign of life on the small island. There was no flag and no empty boxes on the **jetty**.

The landing party entered the **deserted** lighthouse. The clock had stopped, the fire was out and the three men who should have been on duty were missing.

jetty   small pier or platform that juts into water for the mooring of boats

GHOSTLY IN THE COLD SUNLIGHT

There were no signs of violence in the lighthouse. The main room was clean and tidy. There was food in the cupboards and everything was as it should have been.

There were no **oilskins** hanging up. That was odd because all three men would not normally go outside at the same time.

A bad storm had struck two weeks before. The log for 12 December said:

'Waves very high. Tearing at lighthouse. Storm still raging, cannot go out.'

The last entry in the log was three days later on 15 December:

'1 p.m. Storm ended, sea calm.'

That was the last that was heard of the three lighthouse keepers.

WHERE DID THEY GO?

Some said the men had been turned into crows by an ancient **curse**. Others told strange tales of skeleton pirates carrying them away. UFOs are reported in this part of the world. Did aliens carry off the men? Or were all three men washed away by a freak wave?

oilskin   waterproof suit

HUNTING FOR CLUES

If the *Waratah* sank, nobody can guess where. Searches with submarines have tried to find it. In 1999, a team found a wreck. The world waited for news and the report came: 'The wreck is not, repeat not the *Waratah*.' Maybe one day the *Waratah* will be found.

> Divers can find it difficult to identify a wreck underwater.

WHAT HAPPENED TO THE *WARATAH*?

The great new **steamship** the *Waratah* was said to be unsinkable. But one of the big mysteries of the sea is 'where did the *Waratah* go?' No one knows why it disappeared. Despite many searches, the ship has never been found.

On its return **maiden voyage** from Sydney, Australia to London, England the ship vanished. It disappeared somewhere in the Indian Ocean off the coast of South Africa. It left the port of Durban in South Africa on 26 July 1909. On board were 119 crew and the 92 passengers who had not stayed in Australia. It was unlucky for these passengers that they did not stay, as something mysterious happened. To this day, nobody knows what.

> This map shows the route of the *Waratah*. The X marks the spot where it vanished.

gale   storm with very high winds
maiden voyage   first journey

WARNING

Claude Sawyer was a passenger on the *Waratah*. The ship was comfortable and the three-month journey was passing without any problems. But one night Claude had a bad dream. Just before the ship arrived at Durban, he felt something terrible was about to happen. He sensed that the ship was **unstable,** so he got off at Durban and sent a cable to his wife in London.

```
THOUGHT WARATAH TOP-HEAVY.
LANDED IN DURBAN.
```

No one listened to his warning. The great ship sailed on without him. He watched the last thin trail of smoke... and it vanished from sight forever.

A painting of the *Waratah*.

Reports said the *Waratah* must have sunk in a bad **gale**. There were other ideas as well. Had it been sucked down by a huge **whirlpool**? There were stories about shipwrecked children, lifebelts washed up in Australia and messages in bottles. None is likely to be true.

unstable   not steady, unsafe
whirlpool   powerful circular current in the sea

THE BERMUDA TRIANGLE

The ocean has more than its share of 'missing mysteries'. Hundreds of people vanish at sea each year. One area has a very bad reputation for swallowing people up. The Bermuda Triangle sends a shiver down the spines of many sailors.

A TERRIFYING RECORD

The sea between Florida, the Bahamas and Cuba holds strange secrets. In the past 100 years, more than 20 planes and 50 ships have been lost in the Bermuda Triangle. Nothing has been found of them, or of about a thousand people who disappeared. Other parts of the world's oceans also seem to have more than their share of disappearances. These areas are sometimes called Devil's Triangles.

Over 50 ships have vanished in the Bermuda Triangle. **‹‹**

air traffic control   people and equipment that monitor and instruct aircraft in the sky

ONLY NATURAL

The Bermuda Triangle may be a **myth**. Some people say the disappearances are just accidents. They say they are caused by bad sailors who do not know the area. The calm waters around Bermuda might fool them. These are some of the world's busiest shipping lanes, so there are bound to be a few losses. But why do planes go missing as well? Why is wreckage rarely found?

MISSING FOR TEN MINUTES

Perhaps time gets lost in the Bermuda Triangle. A Boeing 727 once disappeared from radar screens and **air traffic control** feared the worst. But the plane landed safely ten minutes later. The crew said they had flown through fog. But their clocks were now ten minutes slow.

GETTING LOST

Perhaps ships could get sucked into a whirlpool. But what about planes?

The Gulf Stream is a strong ocean current off the east coast of the USA. Around Bermuda it may drag boats hundreds of miles off course. The unusual **magnetism** in this area might make matters worse. Add some fog, a freak wave or a **whirlpool** and who knows?

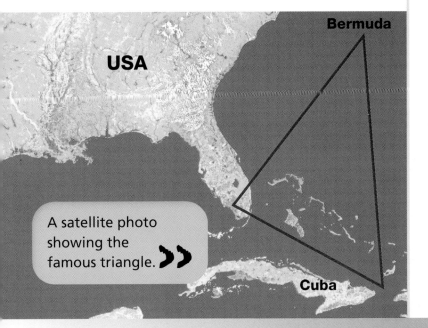

USA

Bermuda

Cuba

A satellite photo showing the famous triangle. >>

magnetism   force that makes a ship's compass point north
supernatural   forces beyond the laws of nature

INSIDE THE BERMUDA TRIANGLE IN 1881

The *Ellen Austin* was sailing from London to New York when its crew saw a drifting ship. Six of them went aboard and sailed in the empty ship as fog fell around them. The next day, the mystery ship had gone. So had the six men. They were never seen again.

NEVER SEEN AGAIN

One of the most famous mysteries of the Bermuda Triangle was in 1963. A huge **tanker**, the *Sulphur Queen*, simply vanished along with its 39 crew.

Two weeks before its last voyage, inspectors checked the *Sulphur Queen* for safety. The ship passed with flying colours. There were new lifebelts and all the lifeboats had been repaired. All its radios were in full working order. Everything was ship-shape, yet the ship disappeared without warning in the Bermuda Triangle. It failed to arrive in port. Then, on 7 February, the coastguard was told the news: *Sulphur Queen* missing.

Just a year later in 1964, the term 'Bermuda Triangle' was used for the first time.

When the *Sulphur Queen* vanished, only debris was left floating in the sea.

debris   scattered remains
SOS   distress signal, short for Save Our Souls

HOPELESS SEARCH

Rescue teams searched 906,500 square kilometres (350,000 square miles) of sea and failed to find any clues. What had happened to the *Sulphur Queen*? How can you lose a huge tanker? Why had there been no **SOS** signal?

Days later a foghorn was seen floating in the sea. Then a ship's name board with '*Marine Sulphur Queen*' written on it was picked up. A few torn life jackets in the sea looked as if sharks had attacked them.

Had the **sulphur** on board the ship exploded? Experts tested the **debris** and there was no sign of fire or sulphur. It still remains one of the Bermuda Triangle's deepest mysteries.

CARRIED BY CURRENTS

In 1991, Michael Plant set off in his small powerboat, *Coyote*. Near Bermuda, he reported something strange. He kept losing electrical power and his long-range radio was not working. No more was heard from him. Months later, his boat was found upside down miles away. Michael was never found.

Coastguards examine the torn life jackets and fog horn – all that was left of the *Sulphur Queen*.

---

sulphur   yellow mineral used to make gunpowder and matches

21

WHERE IS FLIGHT 19?

In 1991 five crashed planes were found in 200 metres of water off the coast of Florida. Divers later proved that these were not from Flight 19. The final resting place of the planes and their crews is still the Bermuda Triangle's secret.

The beauty of the Bermuda area hides its real dangers.

THE DISAPPEARANCE OF FLIGHT 19

The story of 27 men and six planes that disappeared in the Bermuda Triangle has puzzled the world for years. How and why they vanished one day at the end of 1945 is a mystery. Was it the **curse** of the Bermuda Triangle or just human error?

LEARNER PILOTS

On 5 December 1945, five bombers flew from the Fort Lauderdale Naval Air Station in Florida on a training flight over the sea. Charles Taylor was the pilot in charge of 13 student airmen. He was in constant radio contact with all his fellow pilots. Over an hour into the flight, Taylor said his compass was not working. He was not sure where they were.

fate   events that a person has no control over

FROM BAD TO WORSE

The weather grew worse. It was hard to see and the pilots were lost. They began to argue about which way to go. Taylor said he was right and they should fly east. Their planes were running out of fuel, the sea was getting rough and darkness was falling. They still had no idea where they were.

SILENCE

The last signal from Flight 19 was heard at 7:04 p.m. After that the radios went dead. Planes searched the area all that night and the next day. There was no sign of the five missing planes. The **fate** of the 14 men was never explained.

THE OTHER MYSTERY LOSS

To make matters worse, one of the rescue planes also disappeared hours later. It had 13 men on board and there was no distress signal. It simply vanished. A report said that one of the crew had been smoking – which may have blown up the aircraft.

Perhaps the bombers exploded. But there were no signs of wreckage in the sea.

MORE DEVIL'S TRIANGLES

TRIANGLE OF DANGER

On the other side of the world from the Bermuda Triangle is another area of sea with many secrets. Danger **lurks** in the Dragon's Triangle. It is in the Pacific Ocean between Japan, Taiwan and the island of Guam. Many ships and planes have gone missing there.

THE DRAGON'S TRIANGLE

The Dragon's Triangle between Japan and Indonesia is another area of mysterious sea. It is on the Pacific **Ring of Fire** where earthquakes strike. **Seaquakes** can cause giant waves. If a volcano erupts under the sea, the waves will bubble and steam.

Islands have formed overnight in the Dragon's Triangle when **lava** has rushed up from the **seabed**. Old maps show islands that no longer exist because earthquakes destroyed them.

The seabed here drops down miles to the deepest ocean **trenches** in the world. This can make strong currents and **whirlpools**. Sudden fogs and mini-hurricanes are common. So it is not the safest place to sail a small boat!

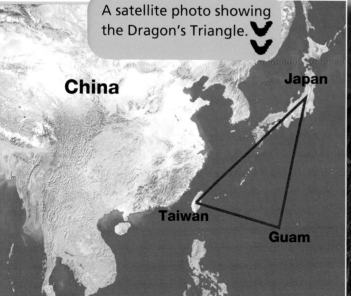

A satellite photo showing the Dragon's Triangle. ❱❱

China

Japan

Taiwan

Guam

WEIRD WORDS

lava   hot melted rock that comes out of volcanoes
lurk   wait around, ready to strike

THE DRAGON STIRS

Like the Bermuda Triangle, this area has strange **magnetic** powers. A ship's compass can often fail and sailors easily get lost in the Dragon's Triangle. For over a thousand years, the Japanese have told of strange disappearances. Old tales tell of restless dragons coming up from the sea to drag sailors down to undersea caves.

Yet it was not until the 1960s that the world began to take notice of the Dragon's Triangle. The news of lost boats began to make people wonder what was going on.

A huge Norwegian **tanker** vanished in 1975. The *Berge Istra* sank in minutes after the radio officer reported that the weather and sea were fine. No **trace** of the ship was ever found.

LOST SUBMARINES

Between 1968 and 1986, 13 Russian submarines were lost in the Dragon's Triangle. Hundreds of men died over a period of 18 years.

What happened? The reasons were not always known. Sometimes it was fire or explosions. But other times, there seemed to be no reason why the submarines should disappear.

Myths about the Dragon's Triangle were based on real dragons!

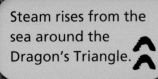

Steam rises from the sea around the Dragon's Triangle.

seabed   floor at the bottom of the sea
seaquake   earthquake under the sea

THE *PATANELA*

A large yacht and its crew of four went missing between Portland and Sydney in 1988. Its **skipper** was skilful and the equipment on board was the very latest. The police thought another boat had hit the *Patanela* – yet no wreckage was ever found.

BASS STRAIT TRIANGLE

For years sailors have told of strange things in the stretch of sea between Australia and Tasmania. Many people think the Bass Strait is Australia's own Bermuda Triangle. More ships and planes have vanished here than along the rest of the Australian coast. Perhaps it is due to the strong **tides**. It could be the **gales** or the shifting **seabed**. Or is it just down to poor ships and sailors? Some sailors say there are more **sinister** powers at work in the sea here.

The *Glasgow Citizen* was a ship full of gold diggers. It left Melbourne in 1862 for Dunedin in New Zealand, but it disappeared forever in the Bass Strait.

Mysteries lurk off the beautiful Victoria coast.

This map shows the position of the Bass Strait.

Darwin•

Australia

Brisbane•

Adelaide• •Sydney
Canberra
Melbourne•
Portland•
Bass Strait

Tasmania
•Hobart

WEIRD WORDS

sinister harmful or just plain evil
skipper person in charge of a boat

THE VANISHING PILOT

Frederick Valentich was a 20-year-old pilot. One evening in 1978 he flew a small aircraft into the sky over the state of Victoria, Australia. He headed out over the Bass Strait. Suddenly radio contact began to fail. It sounded as if the engine was **stalling**. Frederick shouted his very last words into the radio at 7:12 p.m. on 21 October, 'An unknown aircraft is hovering on top of me...' Then the radio went dead. Frederick and the plane were never found.

Another light aircraft disappeared nearby in the same year. People spoke of UFOs and strange lights. But the mysteries are still unsolved.

SIX MINUTES BEFORE THE RADIO WENT DEAD...

19:06 hours

Valentich: Melbourne, is there any known traffic below five thousand feet?

Melbourne: No known traffic.

Valentich: There seems to be a large aircraft below five thousand.

Melbourne: What type of aircraft is it?

Valentich: It's four bright... it seems to me like landing lights...

What happened to the light aircraft that vanished in the Bass Strait?

stalling   coming to a stop
tide   daily rise and fall of the sea

KIDNAP OR MURDER?

PANCHO VILLA

Ambrose Bierce was a famous American writer. He was known all over the USA for his novels and work in newspapers. He set off for Mexico in 1913, when he was 71. Some people said he went to meet a Mexican **rebel** called Pancho Villa who was known to be **violent**. Nobody really knows what happened, but Ambrose Bierce was never seen again.

There were many stories. Some thought he died in the Grand Canyon. Others said he was shot by Pancho Villa or killed in a battle. Maybe he just lived to be a very old man in secret! We are unlikely to find the truth now.

Pancho Villa and his gang may have shot Ambrose Bierce.

Pancho Villa was a hero to some and a villain to others. He and his gang were outlaws who killed Mexican soldiers. They were said to help the poor and steal cattle to sell over the US border. Pancho Villa was killed in 1923.

Ambrose Bierce before he disappeared.

lifestyle   way people live and spend their free time
Manhattan   district of New York

THE FAMOUS JUDGE

At one time Judge Crater was a very popular man in New York City. He was good at his job. He was also rich. His exciting **lifestyle** made him something of a star in the city. The 41-year-old lawyer loved yachts, fast cars and beautiful women. But on the evening of 6 August 1930, he disappeared. One minute he was laughing with friends outside a **Manhattan** restaurant. Then he got into a cab and was never seen again.

The biggest manhunt in New York history followed his disappearance. The search lasted for years and cost millions of dollars. But the mystery of Judge Crater still remains unsolved.

WHAT THE PAPERS SAID ABOUT JUDGE CRATER

KIDNAPPED AND MURDERED!

Judge was involved in crime

Crater lost his memory

he ran away with a secret girlfriend and his missing bank box...

After nine years, Judge Crater was **declared** dead. But reports that he was still alive appeared up to 60 years later.

Lucky Blackiet led the search for Judge Crater. Here he holds a picture of the missing man. **‹‹**

rebel   fighter against the government
violent   using dangerous force

One of the last photos of the Tsar and his family.

THE RUSSIAN ROYALS

The missing remains of the Russian royal family were thought to be hidden down a well. In 1991 some skeletons were dug up and their **DNA** was tested. At last this proved the bones belonged to the royal family. Yet mystery remains. The bones of Alexei and Anastasia were not there.

RUSSIAN MYSTERY

The story of the Russian royal family was a **tragic** one. It was also full of mystery. Their disappearance was one of the secrets of the 20th century.

Nicholas was like a king but was called a **tsar**. He ruled all of Russia. He and his wife, Alexandra, had four girls and one boy. The youngest girl was Anastasia. Her younger brother Alexei was born in 1904. By 1914 Russia was caught up in World War One. Millions were killed in the war and Russia was in a bad way. Some people blamed Tsar Nicholas for being a bad leader. They started to plot against him.

This palace room is where the Russian royal family were executed.

house arrest   being kept prisoner in an ordinary house
tragic   sad and terrible, with an unhappy ending

THE REVOLUTION

The Russian people had no food. While they starved, the royal family carried on living in their rich palace. Workers began to riot and so did the army. In 1917 soldiers threw out the royal family and sent them to Siberia. They were under **house arrest** for 78 days. On the night of 18 July 1918, the royal family was told to go into the cellar with their servants and pets.

Armed men burst in and gunshots were fired. The rest was a mystery. Was the whole family killed? No one knew what happened to their bodies. The world could only guess and fear the worst. The guessing has gone on ever since.

ANASTASIA

Perhaps Anastasia **survived** the bullets because they bounced off diamonds in her clothes. She may have escaped.

Years later a woman called Anna Anderson said she was Anastasia. People were not sure. She married an American and died in 1984 at the age of 83.

Anastasia's story was the biggest mystery of all. ❮❮

THE DINGO – WILD DOG OF AUSTRALIA

AUSTRALIAN MYSTERY

Lindy and Michael Chamberlain were camping near Uluru (Ayer's Rock) in Central Australia. Two of their children were asleep in the tent.

Their daughter Azaria was just ten weeks old. It was August 1980. Lindy looked up into the night sky from the barbecue where she was cooking. It was then she thought she heard a cry. Perhaps it was the baby in the tent. Lindy decided to go and check on her.

Dingoes have been known to attack animals as large as kangaroos.

A dingo is the size of a large pet dog. They sometimes hunt in packs. Dingoes rarely attack people, but some have killed children. Dingoes are now rare in most areas of Australia.

Lindy and Michael Chamberlain leaving Alice Springs court after Lindy was charged with murder.

TERROR

When Lindy got to the tent, she saw a large dingo coming out. It seemed to be dragging something along. She could not see what it was at first. But then the full horror hit her.

WORLD NEWS

Lindy ran into the tent to find Azaria missing. She screamed into the night, 'A dingo took my baby!'

A search found nothing. Azaria was never seen again. But a deeper mystery soon hit the news and **rumours** began to spread. Nobody believed a dingo would steal a baby. There was something odd about this whole story.

The police had doubts. They began to think that Lindy had killed her own baby. She was **arrested** and charged. The trial made world news and Lindy was found guilty. Years later she was set free because of people's doubts. The world will never be sure what really happened to baby Azaria.

THE TRIAL

In October 1982, Lindy Chamberlain was sent to prison for killing her baby. Many people thought it was wrong. There was no real proof. After a 6-year fight, Lindy was set free. Who or what took Azaria remains a real mystery.

The Chamberlains' tent, in front of Ayer's Rock, where baby Azaria disappeared. >>

ACCIDENT OR MORE?

GEORGE LEIGH MALLORY

Mallory was the only climber to take part in all three of the British climbs of Everest in the 1920s. He was born in 1886 and disappeared just before his 38th birthday. He was married with three small children. His family never really knew what happened to him.

At 8848 metres, Mount Everest is the highest point on the Earth. Every climber dreamed of standing on its **summit**, until Edmund Hillary and Tenzig Norgay did so in 1953. They were the first men to get there – perhaps. That was part of the mountain's mystery for many years.

EVEREST MYSTERY

In 1924 George Mallory and Andrew Irvine tried to climb Everest. A climber far below spotted them when they were almost 300 metres from the top. Then heavy clouds came down. The two climbers vanished from sight. They never returned. Irvine's ice axe was found later. But the question was, were they the first to reach the top before they disappeared?

We will never know if Mallory reached the top of Everest.

cruel   unkind and ruthless, taking delight in someone's suffering

75 YEARS LATER

For years, people could only guess what happened to the two climbers. Did they fall or freeze to death? Would they ever be found? Many climbers have been lost in terrible snowstorms on this **cruel** mountain.

Some answers came in May 1999. A party of climbers found a body about 600 metres from the top. They thought it must have been Mallory and they gave him a proper burial. **DNA** tests later proved the body was Mallory. But the mystery of his last hours still remained. Did he ever reach the top? Was he going up the mountain or coming down? Irvine has never been found. Everest still keeps its secrets.

CLIMBING EVEREST

Thirty years after Mallory and Irvine went missing on Everest, Edmund Hillary and Tenzig Norgay stood on its summit. Since then, many other climbers have reached the top. Mallory's grandson, George Mallory II, reached Mount Everest's summit in 1995.

These snow goggles were found in Mallory's pocket when his body was recovered in 1999. ∨∨

summit   very top of a mountain

STORIES

Many tales spread about Glen and Bessie Hyde.

- Did they have a fight and leave each other to start new lives?
- Did they find the trip too difficult and give up secretly?
- Did they fall in the river to be swept away for ever?

GRAND CANYON MYSTERY

When a couple went missing on their honeymoon in the Grand Canyon, a massive search was launched. The Grand Canyon in Colorado, USA, is a steep **gorge**. It is more than 300 kilometres (over 200 miles) long and more than a kilometre deep. It has never revealed the truth about Glen and Bessie Hyde. It probably never will.

MISSING NEWLY-WEDS

Glen and Bessie got married in November 1928. As a special honeymoon, they went **white-water rafting**. The Colorado River roars down the Grand Canyon. This would have been a real **challenge** for their home-made boat. Bessie Hyde wanted them to go down in history as the first couple to tackle the **rapids** right through the Grand Canyon.

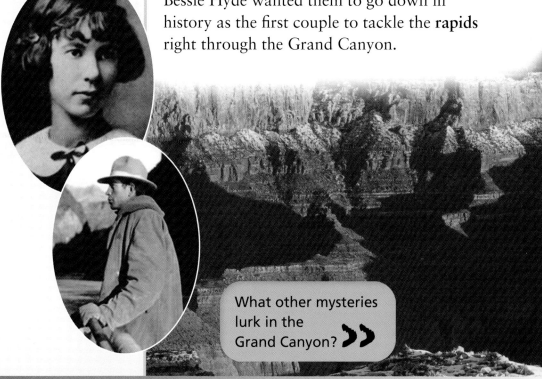

What other mysteries lurk in the Grand Canyon? ❯❯

destination   place where a journey ends
gorge   deep rocky ravine carved by a river

NO SIGN

It seems that they almost made it. A month later, their boat was found floating in calm water. Inside it were a diary, a gun, clothes and boots. The boat was just 75 kilometres (46 miles) from their **destination**. It seemed they had not made it as the first couple to ride the length of the Grand Canyon. The Hydes had just vanished. No **trace** of them was ever found. It was feared they had both drowned. The tale of the Hydes became a popular ghost story among river guides on the canyon. Their story was another mystery of the missing.

THE STRANGER

An old woman joined a Grand Canyon tour in 1971. She said she was Bessie Hyde. She said she had killed her husband before hiking off in 1928. A skeleton with a bullet in the skull was found in the canyon, but it was not Glen. The old woman was not seen again.

white-water rafting riding down a fast-flowing river in a boat or canoe

1937

"

I have a feeling that there is just about one more good flight left in my system and I hope this trip is it. Anyway when I have finished this job, I mean to give up long-distance stunt flying.

"

Amelia in 1937.

PACIFIC OCEAN MYSTERY

The name Amelia Earhart was famous all around the world. She was born in Kansas, USA in 1897. By the 1930s, she was a star. She was famous for flying aeroplanes. Amelia was a brilliant pilot who showed that it was not just men who could fly solo. Everyone wanted to meet her.

WORLD FAMOUS

Amelia wrote books about her travels and set many flight records. In 1932 she was the first woman to fly solo across the Atlantic Ocean. That was an amazing achievement in the early days of aircraft. Then in 1935 she flew across the Pacific Ocean. Such a long flight was unheard of before then.

This map show Amelia Earhart's last flight and the place where her plane disappeared.

equator   line running around the middle of the Earth

ATTEMPT TO FLY AROUND THE WORLD

Amelia wanted to become even more famous. She wanted to be the first woman to fly right around the world, along the **equator**. Such a long flight was a dangerous **challenge**. Everyone thought she was very brave. But her name was to be linked with mystery, too.

Amelia and her **navigator**, Fred Noonan, set off on their daring journey. While Amelia flew her Electra plane, Fred sat in the back with the maps. They covered thousands of miles. They were flying over the Pacific Ocean in the early hours of 3 July 1937 when they lost radio contact. It was near the Dragon's Triangle. They and their plane were never found.

RUMOURS

People even wondered if Amelia Earhart:

- was on a spy mission and was caught
- was held by the Japanese during the war
- ran away with Fred, her navigator
- lived for years on an island in the South Pacific with a native fisherman.

Amelia's Lockheed Electra plane just before take off on her last flight. Amelia and Fred are onboard.

navigator   guide who plans the journey and decides which way to go

LOST AND FOUND

MISSING IN ROMANIA

In 1998, 12-year-old Valentin went missing in Romainia. His parents told the police. A boy had just drowned in the River Danube. Valentin's parents **identified** him and held the funeral. Weeks later, Valentin came back – he had been staying with his aunt. No one knows who they had buried instead!

When someone goes missing for no reason, there is nothing their family can do but worry. If it is not in the person's **character** to go off without telling anyone, you can only wait and hope.

BACK FROM THE DEAD

John Johnson was 69 when he went into the woods to get some logs in 1998. The woods stretched from his home in North Dakota, USA into Canada. He walked too far and got lost in the miles of wild forest. He just could not find his way out again. Eight days later he stumbled on to a road. His family could not believe he was still alive.

John Johnson had eaten lily pads in the forest to survive.

The River Danube produced a new mystery.

character   person's nature or personality

A Narrow Escape

In May 2001, a student climbed down an old mine in Somerset in England. He fell and pulled the rope down with him. There was no way he could climb out again.

For 11 long days he had to lie in the dark and wet. His family did not know where he was. He was miles from anywhere and it seemed hopeless. Then by chance, some children came bird watching. He called out when he heard them. They ran to get help but it took three hours to get him out of the mine. He went to hospital and was soon back on his feet – instead of being another vanishing mystery.

MISSING IN UTAH

Aron Ralston went missing for five days in May 2003. He had gone hiking alone in Utah when a boulder fell and trapped his arm. He could not get away. It took him hours to cut off his arm using a blunt penknife. He escaped, got home and lived!

BACK FROM THE FOREST

Even people who have been missing for years may still turn up one day. There is always hope.

SHOICHI YOKOI

Shoichi worked as a tailor before World War Two. While he was in the jungle he made clothes from plant **fibres**. He ate coconuts, fruit, snails, eels and rats. After he was found in 1972 he got married and went back to Guam for his honeymoon! He died in 1997 at the age of 82.

MISSING, PRESUMED DEAD

At the end of World War Two in 1945, American forces took over the island of Guam from the Japanese. The island is in the middle of the Pacific Ocean, in the Dragon's Triangle. Japanese soldiers had to **surrender** to the US Army. But some soldiers ran into the jungle to hide.

On 24 January 1972, two hunters found Shoichi Yokoi still hiding in the jungle. He had been missing for 28 years. He still thought the war was going on. His family had no idea he was still alive.

Dense tropical jungle is easy to hide in. Or get lost in...

fibres   threads that can be made into cloth
surrender   give up

ALONE IN THE JUNGLE

The famous story from 1971 of Juliane Koepcke is hard to believe. Everyone thought she was killed when a plane flying from Lima to Cuzco in Peru crashed in the Amazon jungle. The search party found that 91 passengers were killed. No one knew that Juliane had got out alive and was walking through the jungle.

Juliane was 17 years old and was totally lost. She followed a stream. At last the stream led to a river. After walking for ten days, she found some woodmen who saved her. The mystery is how Juliane **survived** both the crash and ten days alone in the jungle.

SEARCHING FOR THE LOST BACKPACKER

Louise Saunders, was 19. In 2002, wearing just a T-shirt, shorts and trainers, she disappeared on Mount Tyson in northern Queensland, Australia. She was lost in thick forest for three days. Then she stumbled out and the mystery of her whereabouts was over!

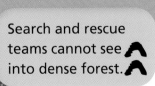

Search and rescue teams cannot see into dense forest.

12 March 2003
Kidnapped girl Elizabeth Smart has been found living just 24 km (15 miles) from her home. Police were called when a woman saw three strange people carrying blankets in the streets of Sandy in Utah. Elizabeth was being held by a **'drifter'** couple, who have now been **arrested**. They used a wig to hide her blonde hair.

BACK IN THE NEWS

Two news stories in 2003 told of different 14-year-old girls who had disappeared. Their families could only wait and hope.

KIDNAP MYSTERY

A gunman kidnapped Elizabeth Smart in the early morning of 5 June 2002. He broke into her Salt Lake City home and took her from the bedroom she shared with her younger sister. Hundreds of people helped to search streets and hills while police followed hundreds of **leads** until the trail ran cold. The news story gripped the nation. Many people feared Elizabeth would never be found alive. Nine months later the police got a call. They rushed to the scene and found Elizabeth safe and well at last.

Elizabeth Smart after she was rescued by police. **《**

WEIRD WORDS   anonymous   from an unknown person
drifter   someone with no real home or fixed address

MURDER VICTIM FOUND ALIVE

A teenage Australian girl was feared dead after being missing for nearly five years. Natasha Ryan was last seen in 1998 when she was driven away by an unknown man. The 14-year-old girl lived in Rockhampton, Queensland. But Natasha was returned to her shocked family after being found in a house nearby in April 2003. A man was already on trial for her murder. Natasha was found with the boyfriend she ran away with in 1998. Police called at a house and found her hiding in a cupboard. She could hardly see as her eyes were not used to the light. She had hardly left the house in four years.

Found after five years

Neighbours next to the house where the missing girl was found said they did not even know a woman was living there. The first hint that 18-year-old Natasha was alive came in an anonymous note to the police.

Posters helped to spread the news of Elizabeth's kidnapping.

Natasha Ryan spent five years in hiding.

KIDNAPPED

Call Police with any information:

Elizabeth A. Smart
14 years old, 5'6", 105 lbs, Blue eyes, Blonde hair.
Abducted from Federal Heights area around 3:00am
June 5,2002

QUITE A HIKE

In 1986 a family moved from Beaver Dam, Wisconsin to Arizona. They took their cat, Sam. The next year they had to move back. Not wanting to uproot Sam again, they left him behind with friends. Guess what? Four years later Sam walked into the house at Wisconsin, 2250 kilometres (1400 miles) away!

BACK FROM NOWHERE

Missing pets can be a real mystery. It is not just where they go that is a puzzle. How do they manage to come back when it seems **impossible**?

MISSING CAT

The Hicks family from Australia had a pet cat called Howie. In 1977, before going off on holiday, they went to the Gold Coast to leave Howie with some relatives. But while they were away Howie went missing. Everyone feared he had been stolen or killed. A year later, Howie turned up back at the Hicks' own home. He had crossed over 1600 kilometres (1000 miles) of Australian desert and wilderness to get there!

It seems impossible that a pet cat could cross the Australian desert...

impossible   cannot happen

MISSING DOGS

Dogs have a habit of going missing, too. Some disappear never to be seen again. They may run away to live in the wild, move in with someone else up the road or get shut in somewhere.

TRAVELLING DOG

In 1979, an Alsatian dog called Nick was stolen when he was on holiday with his owner in Arizona. Somehow Nick escaped and decided he had to get home. But home was 3200 kilometres (2000 miles) away across wild country. He crossed desert, rivers, the Grand Canyon and the 4000-metre-high mountains of Nevada. Four months later he appeared back home in Oregon. That took some doing!

...or that a pet dog could cross a mountain range.

CROSSING THE ROCKIES IN WINTER

In 1923 a collie dog called Bobbie got lost when his owners were on holiday in Indiana. He was 4800 kilometres (3000 miles) from home, but six months later he appeared back home in Oregon! He had crossed rivers and mountains. He was very tired and a bit thin.

47

FACT OR FICTION?

HOW DO YOU EXPLAIN IT?

A few months after David Lang's strange disappearance, his children found a mark in the field. The grass on the spot where their father vanished had turned yellow. It was a circle about 5 metres across. A mystery, indeed!

Flattened grass was the only sign left by David Lang's disappearance.

History is full of weird tales of people who just vanish from the face of the Earth. Are these **legends,** fact or pure fiction? There could be so many explanations.

NO ANSWER

There is a famous story from the USA. It happened in September 1880 at a Tennessee farm near Gallatin. David Lang was walking across a field when he turned to wave to a friend. A few seconds later, in full view of his wife, children and friend, David Lang disappeared in mid-step. They all ran over to him, thinking he had fallen down a hole. Nothing was there. A full search of the farm found no sign of him.

THE MYSTERY OF HANGING ROCK

To the north of Melbourne is a place of mystery. A large rock hangs above the Macedon Range of hills. The locals here talk of 'the lost'. A legend tells how people have climbed the rock never to return. They have vanished forever.

In 1975 Joan Lindsay wrote a book called *Picnic at Hanging Rock*. It tells of a group of schoolgirls who went for a picnic at the rock on Valentine's Day, 1900. Three girls and a teacher disappeared.

People still ask to see the newspaper report about the missing girls at the library in Melbourne. They get upset when they are told it does not exist, as the story was not true!

BENNINGTON, VERMONT – THE SITE OF MYSTERY DISAPPEARANCES

In 1946, Paula Welden vanished on a walk. The 18-year-old was on the Long Trail into Glastonbury Mountain. Someone saw her go behind a rock. When other walkers reached it, she was nowhere to be seen. Paula has not been seen since and no one has a clue where she went.

A scene from *Picnic at Hanging Rock*.

MYSTERIOUS FINDINGS

Things always disappear. There is never much mystery about it. Money, watches, keys – we lose them all the time. They are usually just where we left them. But now and again lost things turn up where we least expect.

MISSING RING

In 1941 a South African woman baked 150 cakes for soldiers in World War Two. She sent them off to the troops, then saw that her wedding ring was missing from her finger. It just so happened that her son was one of the soldiers. He bit into a cake – and there was his own mother's ring. It was soon back on her finger!

18-CARROT GOLD!

Erik Jansson from Sweden lost his gold ring in 1984. He had no idea what had happened to it. Twelve years later he dug up a carrot in his garden. The ring was around the middle of it!

Missing rings can turn up where least expected!

licence   document that gives permission to use or do something

FISHING LICENCE

Ricky Shipman lost his wallet in 1972 near Sunset Beach, North Carolina. He accidently left it in the pocket of his shorts when he was swimming and it fell out and sunk to the **seabed**. He thought he would never find it.

Eleven years later, Ricky's driving **licence** arrived in the mail. A man had found it when he was fishing. The man had caught a large mackerel. When he cut it open, Ricky's driving licence was inside. It was in perfect condition as it was plastic. Ricky's name and address were clear, so he got it back. What are the chances of that happening?

> Be careful what you drop into rivers – it could end up inside your next fish meal.

FISHING FOR TIME

In 1979 a Russian woman dropped her gold watch in a river. Her husband was fishing nearby and he suddenly hooked a large pike. Imagine her joy when he cut open the pike to find her watch still ticking in its stomach!

FIND OUT MORE

ORGANIZATIONS

BERMUDA TRIANGLE
Accounts and records of unexplained events in this area.
bermuda-triangle.org

MISSING PERSONS
The website of the National Missing Persons Helpline lists missing people and stories of those who have been found.
missingpersons.org

AMELIA EARHART
The official website for finding out about this famous pilot.
ameliaearhart.com

BOOKS
Can Science Solve? The Mystery of the Bermuda Triangle, Chris Oxlade and Anita Ganeri (Heinemann Library, 2003)
The Unexplained Pack, (Tick Tock, 2003)

WORLD WIDE WEB
If you want to find out more about mysteries of the disappeared, you can search the Internet using keywords like these:
- 'mysterious disappearances'
- famous + disappearances
- Bermuda Triangle

You can also find your own keywords by using headings or words from this book. Use the search tips opposite to help you find the most useful websites.

SEARCH TIPS

There are billions of pages on the Internet so it can be difficult to find exactly what you are looking for. For example, if you just type in 'water' on a search engine like Google, you will get a list of 19 million web pages. These search skills will help you find useful websites more quickly:

- Know exactly what you want to find out about first

- Use simple keywords instead of whole sentences

- Use two to six keywords in a search, putting the most important words first

- Be precise – only use names of people, places or things

- If you want to find words that go together, put quote marks around them, for example 'urban myth' or 'tarantula myths'

- Use the advanced section of your search engine.

WHERE TO SEARCH

SEARCH ENGINE

A search engine looks through the entire web and lists all the sites that match the words in the search box. It can give thousands of links, but the best matches are at the top of the list, on the first page. Try **bbc.co.uk/search**

SEARCH DIRECTORY

A search directory is more like a library of websites that have been sorted by a person instead of a computer. You can search by keyword or subject and browse through the different sites in the same way you would look through books on a library shelf. A good example is **yahooligans.com**

GLOSSARY

air traffic control   people and equipment that monitor and instruct aircraft in the sky

anonymous   from an unknown person

arrested   held by the police for questioning

assassin   killer who hunts down a victim

automatic   something that works on its own

cabin   room for passengers or crew on an aircraft

cargo   goods carried on a ship or aircraft

challenge   difficult task

character   person's nature or personality

cruel   unkind and ruthless, taking delight in someone's suffering

curse   strange power that is meant to bring harm to some people

database   computer records for fast sorting of information

debris   scattered remains

declared   announced in an official way

deserted   left empty

destination   place where a journey ends

DNA   code locked in our genes that makes us who we are

drama   tense and difficult situation

drifter   someone with no real home or fixed address

equator   line running around the middle of the Earth

fake   not real

fate   event that a person has no control over

fibres   threads that can be made into cloth

gale   storm with very high winds

gorge   deep rocky ravine carved by a river

hold   space in the lower part of a ship for storing the cargo

house arrest   being kept prisoner in an ordinary house

identify   find out someone's name

impossible   cannot happen

jetty   small pier or platform that juts into water for the mooring of boats

lava   hot melted rock that comes out of volcanoes

lead   piece of information that might lead to solving a crime

legend   story based on grains of truth

licence   document that gives permission to use or do something

lifestyle   way people live and spend their free time

54

lurk   wait around, ready to strike

magnetism   force that makes a ship's compass point north

maiden voyage   first journey

Manhattan   district of New York

myth   made-up tale, told over the years and handed on

navigator   guide who plans the journey and decides which way to go

official   according to the rules and records

oilskin   waterproof suit

pressurized   sealed space where the air pressure is controlled

rapids   fast-flowing part of a river with rocks and small waterfalls

rebel   fighter against the government

Ring of Fire   name given to the area of active volcanoes in the Pacific Ocean

rumour   story based on gossip

science fiction   made-up stories that may twist the facts of science

seabed   floor at the bottom of the sea

seaquake   earthquake under the sea

ship's log   diary written up each day by the captain

sinister   harmful or just plain evil

skipper   person in charge of a boat

SOS   distress signal, short for Save Our Souls

stalling   coming to a stop

steamship   large ship with engines driven by steam powered by burning coal

sulphur   yellow mineral used to make gunpowder, matches etc.

summit   very top of a mountain

supernatural   forces beyond the laws of nature

surrender   give up

survive   stay alive

tanker   huge ship for carrying liquid minerals

tide   daily rise and fall of the sea

trace   sign, track or footprint

tragic   sad and terrible, with an unhappy ending

trench   deep ditch, gully or valley

Tsar   emperor of Russia

unstable   not steady, unsafe

victim   person who gets hurt or killed

violent   using dangerous force

whirlpool   powerful circular current in the sea

white-water rafting   riding down a fast-flowing river in a boat or canoe

INDEX

aeroplanes 6–9, 11, 19, 22–3, 27
air traffic control 18–19
arrests 32, 33, 44
Australia 10–11, 26–7, 32–3, 43, 45–6, 49

Berge Istra 25
Bermuda Triangle 18–23, 52
Bierce, Ambrose 28
Briggs, Captain 12–13

Chamberlain, Lindy 32–3
Cooper, Dan 8–9
curses 15, 22

databases 8
dingoes 32–3
divers 16
DNA 8, 30, 35
drownings 10–11, 40

Earhart, Amelia 38–9, 52
Ellen Austin 20
Everest 34–5

gales 17, 26
Grand Canyon 36–7, 47
Guam 24, 42
Gulf Stream 19

Hanging Rock 49
Holt, Harold 10–11
Hyde, Glen and Bessie 36–7

Japanese soldier 42
Johnson, John 40
jungle 42, 43

kidnappings 5, 28–9, 44
Koepcke, Juliane 43

Lang, David 48
lighthouses 14–15

Mallory, George Leigh 34–5
Manhattan 28, 29
Mary Celeste 12–13
Mexican rebels 28
Miller, Glen 10–11
missing persons 4–5, 52
murder 28–9, 30–1, 45

New Zealand 26

pets 46–7
pilots 22, 27, 38–9, 52
Plant, Michael 21
Potter, Jerrold 6–7
powerboats 21

Ralston, Aron 41
rapids 36
Ring of Fire 24
rings 50

Romania 40
Russian royal family 4, 30–1
Ryan, Natasha 45

Salt Lake City 44
seabed 24, 26
seaquakes 24–5
ship's log 13, 15
shipwrecks 16, 17
Smart, Elizabeth 44
SOS 20–1
submarines 11, 16, 25
Sulphur Queen 20–1
supernatural 18–19

tankers 20–1, 25
Triangles 18–27, 39, 42, 52
Tsar of Russia 30–1

UFOs 15, 27
UK 14–15, 41
USA 6–9, 29, 36–7, 44, 46–9, 51
Utah 41

Valentich, Frederick 27
Villa, Pancho 28

Waratah 16–17
Welden, Paula 49
whirlpools 17, 19, 24
World Wide Web 52
Wright, Jackson 6